Just Stop

A BRIEF GUIDE TO RATIONAL THINKING
FOR THE MODERN CONSPIRACY THEORIST

ROSS ELDER

DEDICATED TO ALL THOSE WHO SEEK THE TRUTH, SPEAK THE TRUTH, AND PROMOTE THE TRUTH.

CONTENTS

ACKNOWLEDGMENTS

I can't publish this book without acknowledging several people who were more than instrumental in helping me piece it together. This has also been a puzzle worth solving. First, I will thank YOU, the reader. I was inspired to write this for your benefit after many requests asking how I solve the many puzzles I encounter. If not for you, there would be no outlet for my madness. I also have to thank those who helped create my curious mind – my teachers, instructors, mentors, and coworkers who were instrumental in helping me learn how to become an investigator. I always wanted to be Sherlock Holmes. I have never found one of those damn hats. So, as I age, I become Cannon.

I cannot fail to thank my personal "Laura Holt" who thankfully still sees me as Remington Steele. She is my proof-reader, my sounding board, and is an accomplished investigator in her own right. She is the Mrs. Columbo who may not be seen in the episode, but we always know she's there, giving sound advice to her bumbling detective. She also aids in the use of obscure maritime legal references.

My friends, Ed Gawrelak and Sheila Stephens, both successful detectives, have also been very helpful in assisting me as I navigate the flotsam of internet conspiracies.

INTRODUCTION

My fascination with conspiracy theories began at an early age. As a child growing up across the street from a major U.S. Air Force base, sky watching and imaginatively gazing up at the stars became a frequent distraction as a no-cost hobby. It was the 70s – the age of bell-bottom pants, colorful, strangely-patterned shirts, puffy hair, and disco. UFOs and alien abduction were all the rage; the Watergate conspiracy was still fresh in everyone's minds, and, well, Elvis died. It was a crappy decade all around.

The big thing at that time, and still to this day, was the assassination of JFK in 1963. I was born in the 60s so I was surrounded by people who were alive at the time of the murder and stories of the grassy knoll were plentiful. Nobody was talking about Roswell. Although the supposed UFO crash in New Mexico occurred in 1947, people didn't really start talking about it again until the 90s. No, for my generation, it wasn't so much about JFK or area 51. The big conspiracy of my youth, the one I remember anyway, was the death of Elvis Presley. Was it murder? Did he fake his death in order to escape the endless media coverage and throngs of adoring fans that had followed his every move since the 50s? Ah, those were the days. Things were simple back then.

Then, Al Gore came along. Well, not specifically Al Gore, but whoever the real guy was who created the internet. Suddenly, everyone possessed the capability to communicate with others of a similar mind. The old .bbs bulletin board systems grew into a subculture of whackos and conspiracy theorists who began sharing information about everything from UFO sightings to who *really* killed Kennedy- both of them, and MLK too.

On September 11, 2001, the worst attack on American soil since Pearl Harbor created a unique opportunity for conspiracy theorists from all over the world to discuss, share, fake, and troll, in real time, 24 hours per day. And then stupid happened. Lots of stupid. Seemingly incurable stupid.

My hope, as expressed in this book, is to help prevent you, dear reader, from being a part of that stupid.

CHAPTER ONE: I WANT TO BELIEVE

"It's the repetition of affirmations that leads to belief. And once that belief becomes a deep conviction, things begin to happen."

– Muhammad Ali

"If something is true, no amount of wishful thinking will change it."

- Richard Dawkins

Belief is one of the most powerful mental processes ever developed by the human brain. Belief in a higher power or a fat, bearded, creepy man who sneaks around your house late at night once per year is not required. The simple act of believing something can be a powerful, all-encompassing endeavor. Belief in a cause, such as what drives many of the do-gooders throughout the world, can, almost literally, work miracles in the lives of others. Belief in a form of superiority, such as what drives an equally sizeable segment of the population, can have the opposite effect and cost the world millions of lives. Both believe in something and, once they have latched on to that something, there is no changing their mind.

The same is true of your average conspiracy theorist. They, as a result of their brilliant investigative skills (insert sarcastic tone here), have uncovered something of which the masses are not aware. They possess that knowledge and only they can put the pieces of that puzzle together in such a way that it will make sense. Really, it will make sense. If you would just give them 37.5 hours of your times, they can convince you that all of those puzzle pieces fit together perfectly, almost.

In support of those beliefs, believers often

reference information generated by other believers in order to support their own belief. If you read any book worth mentioning on a conspiracy theory, the theorist will quote from and reference the work of other conspiracy theorists in order to add some sort of imagined credibility to their own work. Richard Belzer, who arguably writes some of the most entertaining conspiracy theory books available, will quote from Jim Marrs and Jesse Ventura, among others, as though those two men possess some level of genius not found in the common man. You become trapped in an endless circle of theorists, all of whom are supporting the overall conspiracy theory with works that often conflict, but are still on the same subject.

Occasionally, they will reference legitimate experts who made vague statements about aspects of a particular case, take those quotes completely out of context, and then shout, "See! I told you so!" But those are rare. It is like the religious believer taking an Einstein quote out of context in order to propose that the last century's best known genius held a deep-rooted belief in god. If you don't read the entire conversation, you can be easily fooled and convinced on the matter. But, alas, Einstein was an atheist, no matter how many single-sentence quotes appear in your church's flier on a Sunday morning.

In case you were still unsure:

"The word god is for me nothing more than the expression and product of human weaknesses, the Bible a collection of honourable, but still primitive legends which are nevertheless pretty childish. No interpretation no matter how subtle can (for me) change this." – Albert Einstein, in a letter to philosopher Eric Gutkind, date unknown.

How many people believed the earth was flat? Galileo Galilei issued his findings that the earth orbits the sun and was summarily convicted of heresy and sentenced to life in prison by the Catholic Church. The Church's beliefs on the workings of the solar system were completely wrong but they believed it anyway and that was all that was necessary for them to impose their belief on others, even to the point of death.

Ancient history, you say? How about just a few decades ago? When I was a high school student, evolution theory had the famous chart below.

From this, the proposed idea was that each version of what was called human evolved from its predecessor. No evidence at the time supported the idea that various species of human coexisted. It wasn't until the 1990s that scientific evidence began to emerge that suggested modern humans roamed the earth at the same time as homo-erectus and the Neanderthal - three separate species, coexisting, perhaps even cooperating for survival. So, after being taught the first theory in school, my understanding of human evolution, and science in general, had to evolve with the times and with emerging evidence. Some people ignore these new revelations and hold on dearly to their original education regardless of how much evidence they are shown. They have latched on to that particular belief and they aren't letting go. This can be applied to any number of beliefs or lessons learned throughout human history.

It is very unlikely you will change the beliefs of a staunchly religious person. Conspiracy theorists possess the same dedication to their particular belief system. The JFK conspiracy crowd is particularly dedicated to their theories, even if those theories change with every new book on the subject. JFK theories are so numerous that no one person could possibly keep them all straight.

Oswald did it, but on behalf of the CIA.

Oswald did it, but on behalf of the Mafia.

Oswald did it, but on behalf of the CIA and the

Mafia.

Oswald did it, but only because he was subjected to MK Ultra mind control.

Oswald did it, but two other guys did it too – from the grassy knoll and the opposite side of the street.

Oswald didn't do it at all. It was someone else.

There were multiple Oswald's and Lee Harvey was just the patsy Oswald.

The Cubans did it.

The Russians did it.

Kennedy was killed because he knew too much about UFOs.

Kennedy was killed because he was too weak on communists.

Kennedy was killed by bankers.

And on and on and on. If you pick up a book on JFK conspiracy, you will be exposed to all of those theories, often within the same book. Richard Belzer, who seems to have dedicated an inordinate amount of time on the JFK assassination, tends to do that in his books on the subject. It seems no conspiracy theory is unworthy of appreciation. But, there comes a time when you have to pick one and roll with it, right? Not really. Apparently, being flexible is a positive trait in the conspiracy world.

Another habit of the JFK crowd is to simultaneously attempt to convince you that the Warren Commission report is a total white-wash while quoting from sections that support their theory in the same breath. It is either correct, or it isn't. It's that simple. You can't have it both ways in the real world but, in the conspiracy world, you can have it seventeen, or eighty five ways and still walk proudly through the crowd at next year's convention.

The Ufology crowd is especially adept at this Dissociative Identity Disorder, what they used to call split/multiple personality disorder, when it comes to information. They will spend days, nay, weeks, convincing you that the government is actively involved in a cover-up with regard to UFOs and that covert government agents are actively distributing disinformation on the subject in order to confuse and divert the UFO investigative community. Then, in virtually the same breath, they will tell you all about the unnamed, anonymous source from within the government who has revealed "X" to them in confidence. So, the government lies about it and is doing its dead-level best to infiltrate the UFO community for the purpose of a disinformation campaign, BUT, now listen to what this government insider has to say. You can't have it both ways.

It starts as a simple, seemingly innocuous virus in the brain. "The official story doesn't sound right to me," or, "Hey, I don't believe that's how it really happened!" Immediately after uttering either of those statements, the brain seems to just melt. Completely. It becomes a mushy sponge that absorbs anything and everything to which it is exposed. I can't explain it. It's a science thing. The O.J. Simpson case would be a good example but I'm not drudging that up again. If you don't want to believe something, no one will be able to convince you. No science will be persuasive and no eye witness testimony will be compelling. You've already set your belief in stone. There are people who still refuse to believe airplanes struck the twin towers.

Once you have chiseled that belief into your cerebral cortex, you see the evidence of your belief everywhere – in every photo, in every video, and in every word not spoken.

Case in point: Ferguson, Missouri, 2014.

Michael Brown, an 18 year old "unarmed black teen," who happened to weigh around 280 pounds and stood 6'4" in height, was shot and killed by Ferguson police officer Darren Wilson during an encounter in broad daylight. Most of you already know the rest of the story but, for those who were living under a rock during the second half of 2014, here are the basics.

Several other criminals, I mean, eye witnesses, immediately told the media that Brown was surrendering, with his hands raised in the air, when Wilson fired 12 rounds, hitting Brown 6 times. "Hands up, don't shoot" became the chant heard all around the world as protests and riots followed the shooting. The media, in its feverish need to promote racial division and create distrust of law enforcement, prosecuted and convicted Officer Wilson of murder every evening during news broadcasts and programs hosted by political hacks who couldn't find a real job. Wilson had to flee Ferguson and hide his family.

But, wait, it gets worse.

A Grand Jury was convened to determine whether Officer Wilson would face charges in Brown's death. Dozens of witnesses were called, piles of forensic evidence was analyzed – a move not common for a Grand Jury – and autopsy results from three separate experts were reviewed. The

Grand Jury found that no murder occurred and that Officer Wilson was guilty of exactly zero crimes related to the incident. They also put an end to the false belief that Brown was in the process of surrendering when he was shot. "Hands up, don't shoot" was a lie. The evidence, the eye-witnesses, the pathology, the blood spatter, the injuries to Officer Wilson – none of it supported the false narrative.

Did that matter to anyone?

Nope.

Ferguson burned for days as riots and looting proceeded just as planned by those who held a belief. A false belief, but a belief none the less. One of the most exhaustive officer involved shooting investigations in recent history, and its findings, meant nothing to those who believed the original story of an attempted surrender and a cold blooded murder. They believed a lie and Ferguson suffered their wrath.

Another fine example from Ferguson, and one in which I have direct knowledge, was the comical antics of InfoWars, Alex Jones' conspiracy theory network that is so successful, it makes most televangelists look like amateurs. Jones is a conspiracy theorist extraordinaire who is best known for his exposure of coffin liners being housed at property leased by a coffin liner company. Oh, and FEMA Death Camps. Those things are everywhere. InfoWars placed two "alternative media journalists" in Ferguson and posted their nightly reports on the various websites affiliated with Jones. While "on the scene" of the end of the world, InfoWars broke the story that Delta Force was also on the scene and god only knows what evil was being planned.

Photographed among the journalists were several rough-looking men dressed in what is commonly referred to as, "tactical attire" such as 5.11 Tactical cargo pants, shooting jackets, ball caps, and camo scarves, or shemaghs, wrapped around their necks. On November 22, 2014,

InfoWars posted the following report:

REPORT: ARMY SPECIAL FORCES IN FERGUSON FOR VERDICT

Men outfitted in suspicious attire appear to provide security for courthouse

Members of a covert military outfit, most likely U.S. Army Delta Force, have been spotted outside the Clayton, Mo., courthouse where a grand jury is convening to decide whether or not to indict a Ferguson police officer.

Infowars reporters on Saturday spotted several men outfitted in suspicious attire and wearing ear pieces in the parking lot of the Clayton courthouse.

Former Army Staff Sergeant and Infowars reporter Joe Biggs, who has carried out multiple tours of duty in Iraq and Afghanistan, reports that the men appeared to be undercover operatives, possibly from Delta Force, due to the way they conducted themselves and their inconspicuous attire.

The operatives arrived in Ferguson in vehicles with North Carolina license plates, which is interesting because Delta Force is stationed in Fort Bragg, North Carolina.

Delta Force was present at the 1993 siege of the Branch Davidian compound in Waco, Texas and at the 1999 World Trade Organization protests in Seattle, Wash.

The nation is waiting to hear whether a grand jury will choose to indict Ferguson police officer Darren Wilson following the August 9 shooting of teenager Michael Brown.

*****

First of all, I've known a few Delta Force operators over the years. They are no amateurs. If they were in Ferguson, you wouldn't know about it. They certainly wouldn't be walking around wearing obvious outfits like those shown in the photos. If

Obama had a son, Delta would probably have looked like that, as opposed to trying to stand out with fashion badassery.

So, who were those spooky, Delta-like goons for the New World Order? They were private security contractors who were hired to escort and protect journalists from the major networks covering the chaos in Ferguson. Some were military veterans and some still serve in the reserve forces but none of them are Delta Force and never were, regardless of what they might tell you if you are a hot, single woman in a bar late at night. I spoke with two of the men myself and have been familiar with them for quite some time because we interact on social media.

Sorry, but this is not the martial law you are looking for. But, if your conspiracy of choice is a military industrial complex plot to create chaos in order to usher in martial law (which is often misspelled in a variety of humorous, and frustrating ways) and the New World Order, you will see it in every action taken by authorities. If police or federal agents happen to be wearing the latest in tactical gear, it is militarization and a part of the plot. If they happen to upgrade their armored vehicles from antiquated tracked-vehicles from the 50s to modern up-armored hummers or MRAPs (Mine Resistant Ambush Protected), obviously they are preparing for an all-out assault on the citizenry. It's so obvious. I don't know how you guys don't see it.

Every person wearing a subdued-in-color scarf will look like a super commando. Every pair of tan boots worn with jeans will be an undercover special ops killer. Every riot will be a false flag operation orchestrated by the government in order to justify the resulting oppression by that same government. You will see what you want to see. Again, facts won't matter. Facts seem to be the only thing conspiracy theorists don't believe in.

ROSS ELDER

CHAPTER TWO: LOOSE MINDS

"Either our government was capable of pulling off the greatest false flag operation in world history; one that involved thousands of people and decades of preplanning and was able to prevent anyone from spilling the beans; or it is a government that couldn't build a working website in three years after spending a billion dollars." – Author unknown

In the aftermath of the horrifying terrorist attacks on the United States in 2001, conspiracy theorists were quick to latch on to this new Pearl Harbor. Conspiracy theories surrounding the original Pearl Harbor attack of December 7th, 1941 had apparently lost their appeal. 9/11/01 afforded junk scientists, pseudo engineers, and slobbering, evangelistic, conspiracy theorists fresh ground upon which to spew their vomit of imaginary information. And then came Dylan Avery.

Dylan Avery, a young man who calls himself a producer, began writing a film script about two American teens who begin investigating the attacks of 9/11 and uncover a secret, government plot behind the attacks. Yes, you read that correctly. It was a movie script. That, in and of itself, should have been enough information to end the discussion of Avery's cheap, poorly produced, poorly narrated "film", Loose Change. We would not be so lucky. Various versions of the film were in the works and Avery's final product, which was actually the second version of the film, was produced in a documentary style. Along with his neighborhood friend, a combat veteran of wars in both Afghanistan and Iraq, these two young men, neither of whom have degrees in engineering, architecture, or explosive demolition, posted version two on

YouTube. The damn thing received over 10,000,000 views in a very short time.

Avery, who himself admitted that he does not believe 9/11 was a government conspiracy in an interview with Mike Spies for Vocativ.com (posted 4/25/2014), soon became a hero to the conspiracy crowd and the poster boy for what became known as the "Truther Movement." Then, after his films and assertions, all of which were based on absolutely no form of science and were inspired by a film script for a work of fiction, he went broke and moved into relative obscurity. Now he's working on a documentary about police brutality. I'm confident his film will be filled with actual facts and will actually involve real people with real expertise upon which to base his findings. *Very confident*. No, not really. I was lying there. I tried to pull that off but it didn't work.

Of course Alex Jones jumped on board with the film and its creators, as did a few celebrities like Charlie Sheen and Alec Baldwin. Before we knew it, the whole internet was generating new theories about how 9/11 happened, or didn't happen, depending upon the "Truther" theory to which you ascribe. Those theories are as numerous, or possibly more so, than even the JFK crowd. Everything from empty, remotely piloted planes being used to no actual planes hitting the buildings at all can be found in Truther theory. Some blame Bush. Some blame the Jews. Most blame everyone except the 19 terrorists who actually committed the act. There seemed to be a very real need for Americans to blame America for the worst attack on U.S. soil in history.

And it was all based on fiction. A lie.

But, Ross, my good man, what about the Architects and Engineers for 9/11 truth? That organization that touts a membership of some 1,400 "experts" who do not believe the government narrative regarding the attacks? Even you, Ross, must give them some form of credence in this investigation! Seriously, they are architects and engineers! Men with letters behind their names on their business cards. Come on!

Bullshit.

I work with architects and engineers quite frequently, and most of them are dumb as a box of rocks. They have an expertise in one thing. One. And it is almost never the designing, building, or demolishing of buildings that are 110 stories tall.

Every time I have seen an interview with someone from Architects and Engineers for truth, it has been someone who is an engineer in a completely unrelated field like communications or electrical engineering, NOT building construction or the precise construction and destruction of something like the WTC complex. A sound engineer working at a radio station in Kuala Lumpur could join the organization. He's an engineer and he believes in the conspiracy and that is all. He is now listed as an engineer, an expert, who supports the assertions of the organization. It is total, and utter bullshit.

When real scientists and real skyscraper construction engineers, demolition experts, and the people involved in the actual design and creation of the WTC complex are interviewed, they support the official story. But they are shunned by any conspiracy theorists because they are obviously just shills for the New World Order. They were bought. They are a disgrace! No, they are the people who actually know what they are talking about and you would appear to be much less of an idiot if you would listen to them and not some bloated, sweating, shouting, conspiracy theorist on a YouTube channel.

It comes down to a predisposition to believe pretty much anything you read, see, or hear. If you are already a paranoid, government hating, conspiracy theorist – perhaps a JFK-type – and then you hear someone using somewhat scientific terminology to describe what they determined was a false flag operation, you are going to just grab on to it and believe it. You are already on the fringe so nothing will seem out of the question for you.

That's why most conspiracy theorists believe in multiple conspiracies or, seemingly, all conspiracies. At times they will be blaming the Masonic Lodge or the Illuminati, while at other times they will blame politicians or the Jews. Blaming a secret agenda is always the end result. Reality is irrelevant. Facts don't matter.

Without exaggeration, hundreds of thousands of people watched the events of 9/11/2001 unfold live on television. Dozens of news organizations maintained live feeds from the moment the first plane struck the building until several days afterward. And yet, there are still theorists out there trying to convince you that not a single plane struck the twin towers or the Pentagon on that Tuesday morning. It is a lie unlike any lie ever told and it is a smear on the entire country that anyone could be as stupid as to believe it. Shockingly, thousands of people do believe it.

We know what happened. We know who perpetrated it. We know who planned it. We know why the buildings fell in the manner in which they collapsed. We know how many people were killed. We know who the villains and the heroes were on that day. The facts are clear.

Loose Change, the fake documentary, led to "loose minds"; people who were willing to buy in to any conspiracy so long as it placed the blame squarely on the U.S. of A. instead of those who were really behind the attack. Those 'people of loose minds' have since spread throughout the worldwide web to use their brilliant powers of deduction on various other so-called conspiracies, such as the Sandy Hook school shooting and the death of journalist Michael Hastings. They see conspiracy everywhere they look because that is what they want to find.

The guy was wearing a shemagh scarf. Know who wears shemagh scarves? Commandos. Therefore, commandos are on the scene. The scarf-wearing commando was seen driving an SUV. Know who drives SUVs? Government agents. The scarf-wearing commando government agent was driving an SUV bearing license plates from the state of North Carolina. Do you know what else is in North Carolina? The Sealy Corporation – manufacturer of fine mattresses. Sealy mattresses are sold globally. It is a global corporation. Who buys a lot of mattresses? FEMA. Obviously, Sealy Corporation is a front company for secret government commandos who prefer to drive to Missouri versus flying coach-class and they are here on behalf of the New World Order to strip you of your rights, brutalize you, imprison you in a FEMA camp, and impose martial law.

And that, my friends, is how a conspiracy theorist thinks.

And then they write that shit down.

And then it spreads throughout the internet like an STD in a Tijuana brothel.

CHAPTER THREE: JUST THINK

"Once you eliminate the impossible, whatever remains, no matter how improbable, must be the truth." – Sir Arthur Conan Doyle, attributed to his most famous detective, Sherlock Holmes

"Facts are stubborn things; and whatever may be our wishes, our inclinations, or the dictates of our passions, they cannot alter the state of facts and evidence." – John Adams, 2nd president of the United States

During the course of my life I have held many occupations. The trade in which I spent the most time, received the most training, and hold the most experience is investigations. Since my teens, while studying criminal justice and watching reruns of

Starsky & Hutch, I have been obsessed with the investigative process and the search for truth. I am considered quite good at the whole thing. To be honest, training only gets you so far in such a field. Experience is key to becoming an experienced investigator. You also have to have a finely-tuned bullshit detector. Without that BS divination tool, you can easily be led down the rabbit hole of falsehoods tracking the wrong person, pursuing the wrong perpetrator, or chasing your tail trying to figure out how an Ewok could have possibly absconded with the bank funds even if he was capable of becoming a ghost and walking through walls. I mean, sure, maybe he can walk through walls but how did the bank bag pass through the wall? It just doesn't make sense.

And there you have it. Even if you can imagine the most ridiculous cause for something, you will eventually come across a piece of the puzzle that doesn't make sense. In the above example, the creature could alter its physical being in order to pass through physical objects. But, so what? You still have to get the bag through the wall and bags are an inanimate object that have neither special powers nor a mind with which to conjure them. Therefore, the bank bag could not alter its physical being in order to pass through the wall. Case closed. Shape-shifting, ghost-like Ewoks simply could not have stolen your bank bag, sir.

There are basically two schools of investigation; one wrong, and one right. The first seems to be popular with TV dramas and any reality TV show about police work. In this method, you search for the most likely suspect and then spend a great deal of time trying to find evidence to support your case against your suspect. This, as you may know, but maybe not, is NOT the way to conduct a proper investigation. Unfortunately, I see this method used far too often in reality as well. You can probably find some in your own area if you follow various police blotters and court cases. This is how people spend decades behind bars for crimes they did not commit.

"I think Bush was behind the whole thing."

Okay, now, let's spend the next three years trying to find links between Bush and Bin Laden and all those Saudi terrorists with pilot training. Well, in some way of weird linkages and references – think six degrees of Kevin Bacon – you probably will find some very tenuous and shaky connections between some of those characters. Next thing you know, you are calling The Hague and trying to have Bush indicted for the use of chemical weapons against the Syrian Army. If you look for something hard enough, you will probably find something that you believe is pertinent and real. It won't be, but you will think that anyway. Refer back to the Sealy commando death-squads piece in the last chapter if you have further questions.

The proper method of conducting an investigation is simple: Follow the available evidence until you find the truth. No preconceived notions, no prejudices, and no predetermined suspects. You allow the crime and the evidence to lead you, the intrepid sleuth, to the perpetrators. It really is that simple but people confuse and convolute the entire process with a variety of issues unrelated to being a good investigator.

And people make mistakes.

Years ago, while working for a major pharmaceutical company, I was asked to assist a young investigator in an embezzlement case. Covert surveillance cameras had previously been installed and this investigator had received all of the important documentary evidence that would make the case quite easy to solve. After reviewing the surveillance footage and comparing notes with the documents and reports, the investigator was stumped. I arrived to find a young man working overtime in an attempt to make sense of it all. He was on the verge of quitting his job due to the inordinate amount of frustration and difficulty.

It seemed that the reports and documents indicated one thing but, when viewing the video footage, the visual evidence seemed to indicate something else completely. He couldn't figure it out. I might have spent hours trying to figure it out myself had I not glanced at my watch to check the date I was about to jot down on an investigation form. Once I looked up at the monitor again, I noticed that the date on the surveillance tape was wrong. He had been watching footage of the wrong day the entire time while attempting to match it up to transaction data on the printed reports. This wasn't his fault, really. The date on the surveillance system was wrong. The reports were dated the 13th and the video footage was dated the 13th but, due to the incorrect dating on the surveillance system, he was actually reviewing footage from the 12th. A simple detail was overlooked that caused several hours of wasted time and unnecessary aggravation. So, we found the correct video, put the pieces together, and then arranged for the detention and interrogation of the subject who promptly confessed.

Mistakes are made all of the time. If you read a report from a first responder who declares that, "The spent casings lying near the body were from 9mm pistol rounds" and then you read the coroner's report that states, "The victim was killed by three

.40 caliber pistol rounds to the torso", did you uncover a conspiracy? Probably not. You discovered an error on the part of one of those people. Most likely, you uncovered an error on the part of the first responder who simply saw shell casings on the ground but did not pick them up to examine them because they were evidence and were not to be disturbed until detectives could collect them and log their exact location within the crime scene. Your typical conspiracy theorist will determine that two different weapons were used in the crime and may even go so far as to claim that it was an attempt to frame the prime suspect. Now, if the first responder says 9mm and the coroner recovers .40 slugs from the corpse and then the only weapon attributed to the prime suspect is a .25 caliber Iver Johnson semi-auto, you may be on to something. But keep digging.

Modern keyboard investigators, which most conspiracy theorists are, lack one vital thing with which to work: Actual evidence. When something happens and police have yet to make an arrest and the case has not gone to court, the evidence isn't just laid out for all to see. The case has to be protected and the person's right to a fair trial, conducted by an impartial jury, must be preserved. The most damning evidence in the case is not going to be released to the public. You can reference the Michael Brown shooting here, if you like. The media and the public were not privy to the entire body of evidence. The Grand Jury in that case DID have access to all evidence and they made the decision that Officer Wilson acted appropriately. Meanwhile, keyboard warriors everywhere were convicting Wilson of a crime by public opinion based on absolutely nothing except the supposed eye-witness testimony of a known criminal who was getting his fifteen minutes of fame by promoting a racial hatred agenda. Hands up, don't shoot – the lie – was the product of a dope smoking shoplifter who ran and hid when Wilson made contact with he and Brown in the street. He wasn't even an eye-witness in that regard, but his false testimony, blasted all over the world, has resulted in massive property damage and injuries all over the country. All of which occurred without a single piece of evidence from which to draw a conclusion.

Most evidence isn't going to be available over the internet at all. You may be able to find small pieces here and there but, if you aren't downloading official documents and testimony of witnesses, you are really taking a risk in the area of truth. How can you solve a crime while sitting in your underwear in your mom's basement with the soundtrack to an Oliver Stone film playing softly in the background? You can't. Most people can't visualize what they are reading. Unless you go to the exact location, at the same time of day, under the same atmospheric conditions that were present during the incident, you can't say definitively that you understand the scene. You have to see it from the perspective of the victim as well as the perpetrator. You have to be standing in that exact spot.

And now for something deeply personal.

During my tour of duty in Afghanistan in 2012, I was involved in several AR 15-6 investigations. For those unfamiliar with military regulations and lingo, a 15-6 is either a formal or informal investigation depending upon the requirements set forth by regulations and command requirements. In essence, it is an investigation into the facts of a certain matter and can range from a suspicion of misconduct to the forensic analysis of a death scene. In Afghanistan at that time, all deaths of U.S. personnel or Afghan civilians required a subsequent AR 15-6 investigation. Since most wartime 15-6 investigations are classified, I cannot reveal the details of those investigations but, using a little creativity, I will give you an idea of the process and results.

In the first case for discussion, a civilian was killed by an armored vehicle, an MRAP, on the only improved road surface in the area. Traffic was light, even by Afghan standards, and visibility and weather conditions were not a factor. (Video footage of the incident was available from a makeshift dash cam arrangement in a vehicle several hundred yards behind the vehicle in question but the view was blocked by an MRAP between the two.) Sworn statements were gathered from all witnesses, civilian and military, and the driver of the vehicle was questioned extensively. Those reports were then forwarded to those who would conduct the investigation. I assisted the two Army Officers assigned to the investigation. In most cases, the Investigating Officer for an official investigation in the military must be an actual officer, although exceptions can be made based on level of expertise and immediate availability. As we reviewed the reports, the evidence just didn't snap in to place like a well-constructed puzzle should. The body's distance from the vehicle, the vehicle's path of travel, and various other aspects of the statements seemed to indicate that someone wasn't telling the whole truth.

When asked for further details, more statements were taken and it got even weirder. We determined that an actual, on scene investigation would have to take place. A standard traffic accident investigation was conducted. Measurements were taken, math was deciphered, and we walked through the incident in the same place as it originally occurred. Then, and only then, did it make sense. Not one person was found to be lying about the incident. Each witness statement was true and correct based upon their perspective and visibility. It was an accident, nothing more.

The second case involved the deaths of U.S. soldiers during a suicide bombing attack. This was a bit more complex and involved the emotions of those involved as well as the emotions of those conducting the investigation. These were people we knew and respected. We had to do this right and bring closure and justice to the situation. It wasn't easy. Much of what was written in witness statements didn't seem to make sense and there were stories of shots being fired and Afghan police shooting civilians. We weren't sure if we had a potential insider attack or just an opportunistic assault by insurgents. Again, we had to go to the scene of the crime.

I heard, and was first to report, the explosion when it happened. Since it was more than a kilometer away, I did not know at the time that it was an attack on personnel conducting a Key Leader Engagement within the village. We speculated that it could have been another failed rocket attack where the rocket landed far outside the walls of our FOB (Forward Operating Base). Using our surveillance assets, we attempted to find smoke, or a crater, or any evidence of a rocket impact. We found nothing in the immediate area. Soon afterward, the radio traffic began.

Initial reports are always sketchy and questionable. People are in the midst of something extraordinary and their minds race with adrenaline, fear, and anger. They say things that later turn out to be untrue. They meant well, but they were trying to put the pieces together on the fly at a time when their own survival is in question. They hear things, misunderstand things, and often confuse innocuous things with threats.

As it was happening, my own reactions were confused as well. How did this happen? What that person just reported isn't possible. Why were they in that location? Dismounted? Why were they dismounted there? It made no sense at the time. Due to the presence of Afghan media personnel, photos and video were available immediately following the attack. Even those did little to reconcile the statements and details we had been given thus far. There was also a math problem. The list of dead and wounded, when compared to the vehicle manifests, didn't match. We had an MIA – an Afghan interpreter.

The MIA factor caused speculation to run rampant among the unit. Was he the bomber? Was he an inside informant for the insurgents who fled the scene to avoid being caught after the attack? These were very serious factors to consider during our investigation. Eventually, he was ruled out among the suspects. We found him. Well, what there was to find. He wasn't identified until DNA analysis was concluded and it was discovered that he had been standing at the epicenter of the explosion. He was essentially vaporized. He was not a criminal but a victim.

When conditions on the ground permitted, we embarked on our journey through the crime scene. I had the distinctly disturbing pleasure of standing in the exact spots where our friends had died, one by one, measuring distances from objects, vehicles, and the apparent "ground zero" of the blast. Again, then, only then, could my mind decipher the puzzle that had plagued me for a couple of days.

"Oh, Jesus. Right there. That's where it happened. He came in from there, between those. They were walking right here, heading for that area." Piece by piece, the scene came together into a coherent picture. The sworn statements became clear.

If I had only the initial reports and witness statements from which to work, I would have reached a very different conclusion. The interpreter signaled to the insurgents and arranged the attack, after which, he fled the area and the Afghan police began firing into the crowd in a brief gun battle with insurgents that left 18 civilians dead.

But, that isn't what happened.

The interpreter was vaporized, the suicide bomber was on a motorcycle, and the police fired their weapons in the air in order to drive the civilians from the area in case there was a follow-on attack by ground forces. All of the dead and wounded, U.S. and Afghan alike, received their wounds from the bomb blast. Partial details will create partial results. This is what the modern internet investigator fails to understand.

Historic examples of this can be found as well. Most so-called researchers of the assassination of JFK use the Zapruder film, a 26 second long film captured by Abraham Zapruder at the time of the assassination, to either support, or refute, the official story. The first thing to realize is that the first 7 seconds of the film are unrelated to the assassination. Zapruder filmed part of the motorcade procession that preceded the President's limousine, then stopped, and then began recording again once the President was in view. Therefore, only 19 seconds of the film are relevant to the assassination.

Contrary to many conspiracy theories, Zapruder was not there to confirm the death or in any way involved. His office was located along the route and he simply stepped out into the plaza to begin filming.

Everyone can agree that the Warren Commission report on the incident was half-assed and did not present or examine much of the evidence. They wanted closure, as did a country still in mourning. But, what they did say was that three bullets were fired. They know one bullet missed the President completely, one passed through both the President and Governor Connally, and the third, and last, struck the President in the head.

Time, Inc. then quickly purchased the rights to the film and, using still frames from the film, issued their Life Magazine "investigation" into the murder.

Time, Inc. is the source of the "*4.8 seconds to 6.3 seconds for all three shots*" theory. Time, Inc. came up with that. Not an actual investigator or a forensics analyst or an expert on assassinations but a group of journalists.

And they were wrong.

Years later, when a true analysis of the films (there were more than the Zapruder film), still photos, eye witness reports, and official statements from those within the motorcade was completed, it was determined that the first shot was the shot that missed the President. That shot occurred BEFORE Zapruder began filming. Looking at the films and stills, when the Zapruder film begins, secret service agents are already responding to something out of the ordinary. One secret service agent, a man named Hickey, in his sworn statement said he thought someone had thrown a firecracker into the plaza. This occurred before the second shot struck the President in the back. Before. Before the film starts.

Analysts believe the first shot struck the mast-arm of a street light and ricocheted into the curb, a piece of the bullet, bullet jacket, or concrete striking a bystander, grazing his cheek.

Oswald was tracking the moving target and pulled the trigger when he thought he had the best opportunity for a hit. He misjudged the movements and the point of aim passed over the mast-arm as he pulled the trigger, causing the bullet to hit the mast-arm and fly off course. Around two seconds later, the Zapruder film begins.

"6 Seconds in Dallas" is, and always has been, a lie. It wasn't an intentional lie, per se. It was simply a poor investigation. Because of the existence of the Zapruder film, the assumption was made that the film captured the assassination in its entirety. It did not. It only captured two of the three shots fired. Extensive analysis of the film by a plethora of experts cannot identify three shots in the film. They can only identify two.

The timeline created by the "real" investigation conducted by experts many years after the fact, gives Oswald 11 seconds to fire the three shots at the President, not a maximum of 6 seconds. That gives you a completely different story than the one that has been believed for more than fifty years. Newsweek.com posted the results of this investigation in an article written by Max Holland on November 20, 2014.

But, but… what about the **broken scope**, Ross? How do you explain **THAT**?

It was determined that the scope on Oswald's Carcano rifle was broken. That much we do know. But, we have no way of knowing if the scope was broken before, during, or after the shooting. The FBI removed the scope while checking the rifle for prints and we have no way of knowing what happened to it during that time. We also don't know how roughly Oswald stowed the rifle in its hiding place after the shooting. It may have been thrown or dropped during that time. But, there is another possible explanation as well.

What if the rifle's scope was broken before the shooting, as theorists like to claim? Does that mean Oswald could not have made the shots?

Nope.

The broken scope actually fits well in the theory of the first missed shot. If the scope was damaged, it would have caused the first shot to go wildly off course, missing the limousine completely, hitting the curb after the ricochet off the street light. Oswald would have recognized that the shot missed wildly and, following his Marine training, would have reverted back to the rifle's iron sights. The type of scope mount on the rifle allowed for full view of the iron sights with the scope mounted. So, he missed the shot prior to Zapruder starting his camera back up, gave up on the scope, and used the iron sights to complete the next two shots.

Even with iron sights, a shot aimed at the torso of a man at a maximum distance of 81 meters, the farthest distance from the window to Kennedy at the point of the impact to Kennedy's head, is not difficult by any means. Oswald was probably aiming high on Kennedy's back and pulled the shot, or the rifle moved as he tracked the target, resulting in the shot going high and hitting the head. Even if he had been aiming at the head itself, iron sights at that distance would be more than adequate to hit the target.

Although the rifle is not accurate by modern standards, which often describes a rifle with a 1-MOA accuracy, or a 1-inch shot group at 100 yards, the Carcano was by no means a "junk" rifle. Even during Warren Commission testing, the Carcano produced shot groups of 3-4 inches at 100 yards.

11 seconds, three shots, a moving target - but a target that is moving away from the shooter, not side to side - iron sights at a distance of less than 100 yards. Those are the facts of the case. I could go down to my local gun range and find several dozen people capable of making those shots and none of them are trained Marines.

This, of course, does not preclude the existence of a conspiracy in relation to JFK's death. It does, however, discredit any conspiracy theory predicated upon the assumption that Oswald *could not* have killed Kennedy.

Just like "Hands Up, Don't Shoot", "Six Seconds in Dallas" was the result of incomplete information, improper investigation, and an agenda driven narrative that became the truth to an uninformed audience. They were lies. One intentional, the other by mistake.

Through Freedom of Information Act requests, browsing public records, and phone calls to various agencies, you can get your hands on many documents pertaining to just about any incident short of an ongoing murder investigation. You will still have only a partial picture of what happened, but it is a better picture than can be found reading news reports and commentary on the issue. If the sum total of your knowledge came from Facebook posts and Tweets, you should just sit down and shut up and please, please don't type anything into that comments field.

ROSS ELDER

CHAPTER FOUR: THE SKEPTIC

"The same principles which at first view lead to skepticism, pursued to a certain point, bring men back to common sense." – George Berkeley

Over the years I have often been accused of being a shill for the opposition, an illuminati insider, and a goon for the New World Order. Although none of those things are true, they do have a root somewhere close to the truth in that I often debunk opinions, ideas, and conspiracies that are found on 'my' side of the aisle.

Why do I do that? It's simple: Because I

expect the opposition to lie to me. I expect the enemy to mislead me. I do not, however, tolerate being misled by those I consider to be on 'my' side. In reality, both ends of the spectrum utilize the same form of charlatanism and shenanigans to manipulate and control their specific group. It makes me angry. So, although I could easily spend all of my time debunking and refuting claims coming from those I consider my opposition, that would do nothing to help my friends, family, and those of a similar mind in their quest to decipher the truth.

People are prone to skepticism when it comes to their opposite party or political philosophy and yet, when confronted by information originating from their own philosophy or party, they fall for it hook, line, and sinker. They shed their skepticism when the information falls in line with their own beliefs.

"Our side said it so I trust the information," they might say. Regardless, they fail to review the information and neglect to perform any kind of research on their own. They just believe it, whether it is true, or not. And that, my friends, is dangerous. Mindless sycophants heading to the voting booth every other year, pulling that no longer present lever in the same fashion every cycle, punching that button that says "R" or "D" without proper education is just as dangerous as any Police State or FEMA plot.

For me, being a skeptic doesn't just mean questioning the motives of those to which I am most often opposed. It means questioning the motives of everyone, questioning the validity of everything, and applying the common sense rule to all things.

I'm sure most conspiracy theorists consider themselves skeptics but they are generally only skeptical of theories other than their own, or those generated by their favorite story teller. Some take it to the extreme and will never believe the official, government information about anything of importance. Body count at a mass shooting? Forget about it! You can't trust the gubmint, man! They are lying to us again! They forget one important piece of the skeptic's puzzle and that is to not become so skeptical that you become delusional.

Sandy Hookers, the moniker given to those who believe the Sandy Hook school shooting never actually happened, are well-known for their idiotic brilliance. They don't have the answer to the first, and most important, question regarding their theory: what purpose would it serve? I know, they will throw out gun control, the police state, and martial law – the same things they throw out for every conspiracy theory. None of them make sense, but that doesn't matter. Part of being a skeptic involves being able to accept the truth. If you don't accept the truth when it is encountered, well, then you aren't a skeptic. You're an idiot. Being a skeptic doesn't mean believing nothing.

A good example of how conspiracy theorists think could be illustrated by examining what, and who, they believe. Let's look at the UFO subject briefly.

Many people who are involved in amateur, and even what would be considered professional research into the UFO question believe certain things and you can't convince them otherwise. For instance, they believe an alien spacecraft crashed in Roswell, New Mexico in June of 1947 and there were several other crashes in the following years. The U.S. government, they believe, has been reverse engineering the found materials and have used that new knowledge to build state of the art aircraft and spacecraft, including deadly weapons with which to ensure U.S. dominance on the world stage.

Within that theory, there are certain individuals who are revered as having been whistle blowers and insiders who have stepped forward to share this "above top secret" information. Bob Lazar is the first to come to mind. Bob claims to have been a nuclear physicist who was recruited to work at Area 51 in Nevada where he was directly involved in reverse engineering the power plants used to power these alien craft. Bob's superior intellect and education, having graduated from both MIT (Massachusetts Institute of Technology) and CIT (California Institute of Technology), convinced people that he was a reliable witness. His work with a world leader in space and aircraft technology also pushed his credibility levels beyond that of mortal man. He was the golden child and, in some circles, remains so.

And, well, Bob is a liar. A bad one. He is a lying liar who lies. He never attended MIT or CIT. His only education was two years at a Junior College and he never worked for those super high speed aerospace companies either. None of it was true, and yet, if you talk to any UFO buff today, twenty years after his appearance on the UFO circuit, you'll be told many fantastic stories that simply must be true because Bob said so.

Ironically, Bob was outed by fellow UFO researcher, and a man who actually IS a nuclear physicist, Stanton Friedman. I guess Friedman got tired of a fraud stealing his thunder at the UFO conventions so he had to shut him up once and for all. Friedman did a background investigation on Lazar and discovered, as he suspected, that everything Lazar claimed was total fabrication. Why did Friedman conduct that investigation? Because he was skeptical. As a nuclear physicist, Friedman knew that many of the things Lazar said didn't make sense. Most people would just acquire a blank expression and attempt to keep their eyes open while someone is discussing physics and as yet undiscovered elements and, since that isn't their area of expertise, they would have no idea Lazar was just spouting off a bunch of speculative and imaginary bullshit. It took an actual physicist to spot the erroneous information and begin the close examination of the presenter.

Timothy Good, a man who has written numerous books on UFOs, Roswell, and government cover-ups of alien visitations, eventually had to publicly announce that much of what he had written on the subjects were complete hogwash. Not because he was intentionally misleading people, but because most of his information was acquired from a government insider who, in a strange twist, worked for Air Force counter intelligence and was providing the bogus information as part of a disinformation campaign. You see, the USAF didn't like people snooping around their top secret projects so, in order to keep them on the wrong scent, USAF OSI agents were assigned the task of seeding, and manipulating information for distribution throughout the UFO community in order to keep them looking for little green men instead of figuring out the latest air craft designs.

You can learn about this disinformation campaign, and see Good's public admission, in a fascinating documentary titled, The Mirage Men. I highly recommend it.

The list goes on and on but I think you get the idea. The bottom line is that they are only skeptical of those who do not hold similar views. In order to be a well-rounded skeptic, you have to be skeptical of information that seems to fit together just a bit too well. Does it perfectly align with the currently acceptable narrative? You should question that. Life is messy. Nothing is perfect, generally, unless you are talking about Natalie Portman. Don't tell her I said that.

Being skeptical is the first step in not being fooled, whether it is by your opposition or your own camp. Before you leap into a theory or position, just spend a little time researching it. As I tell my children, today's computers and the ever expanding internet places all of the knowledge of the world at your fingertips. Literally. Almost everything that has ever been written can be found with a few keystrokes and some bandwidth. There is no excuse for not understanding something today. None.

And we see it every day. You saw it today if you were on any social media websites. Follow with me. You will see what I mean. Let's say you are a member of a few pro-gun groups on, let's say, Facebook. Now, your newsfeed scrolls and scrolls and then you come upon a post in your aforementioned gun group that asks, "Why are my shots hitting low and to the left all the time?"

If you are a gun person, you will begin smacking your forehead into the keyboard of your laptop. Why? Because that question has existed since people started keeping track of their bullet impacts. It has been answered as many times as it has been asked. If you search those words on Bing or Google, you'll get millions of hits. Millions.

Well, specifically, when I input those exact words on my google search field, it returned 2,380,000 results. If the person has the time to ask that question in a group on social media, they had the time to ask that question on an internet search engine and figure out the answer themselves. But, they didn't. And now thousands of people are slamming their heads against computers, tables, and walls.

Those are the kinds of people who blindly click the "share" button on posts without reading beyond the headline. Someone of relative importance posted it, so they share it and have absolutely no understanding of the post's truthfulness. If they did take the time to read it prior to hitting the "share" button, they just accepted it as the gospel because it was posted by someone they trust.

Trust is dangerous.

Trust, but verify, is intelligent. If it was good

enough for Ron Reagan, it is good enough for me. Therefore, that is the skeptical approach I take in my day to day life. It doesn't matter if the post is from someone I admire or respect. If I don't know if the information is factual, I research it myself before helping spread it across social media. People, even intelligent and well-meaning people, can be fooled. It isn't just the semi-literate mouth breathers who can be sucked in and misinformed. One informed of the mistake, a well-meaning person will remove the post or write a retraction. That isn't the case with those committed to their agenda.

On many occasions, after finding an erroneous story or post on someone's social media (including politicians, actors, and writers) I have posted a rebuttal or debunking article within the comments of the questionable post. More times than not, I get attacked, and that scares me a little. It scares me that someone can be so firmly dedicated to a lie that they will actually threaten physical harm to those who oppose their point of view. Now, am I actually afraid of physical harm? No, not at all. The point is that, even when confronted with the truth, there are those who don't care. They will continue promoting the lie. I find this most often with political posts and anything anti-Obama. It doesn't matter if it is true. If it supports a hatred toward the target, it is considered fair. It has become the smear campaign and mud-slinging fest that used to be confined to television ads in the south.

As with the poor trigger control and recoil anticipation post in the gun group, the truth surrounding many of these memes, viral videos, and incriminating photos is usually easily accessible. A copy of an image can be posted to google and matching photos can be located. That will tell you when a photo was taken, or at least when it was first posted to the internet. It can also show results for similar photos. This is helpful if you believe a photo was altered using software such as Photo Shop. There are also photo forensics websites that allow you to upload a photo for free analysis. Faked and altered photos are pretty easy to spot using these tools.

Below is an example of how twisted some people can be in the realm of photo alteration. Perhaps this was done as a form of humor, or maybe the person is just a major racist and that is how they feel. Regardless, guess which photo spread across social media like a plague? Yep, the fake one. This photo was shared by hundreds of thousands of people across the internet who believed that some guy was actually standing at a protest holding a sign defending armed robbery. Does that even make sense? No, but that didn't stop people from sharing it and claiming it is real.

Some friends and I debunked this one in a matter of minutes using the Google Images search feature. Sarah Rustle, a social media friend, put the photos together to show the truth of the matter. The original source of the photos is unknown.

If you are a racially motivated person who believes all black people are thugs, criminals, and miscreants who spend all day trying to find new ways to rob people, the altered version of the photo makes perfect sense. You probably shared it on your Facebook page. If you are a normal human being with a healthy degree of skepticism, and perhaps a little bit of intelligence, you saw the photo and thought, "Wait a damn minute. That can't be right." Your instincts were correct. You should have no difficulty looking yourself in the mirror in the morning. Those who shared it without hesitation, however, may need to do a little self-reflection. You are a bigoted jackass. Change. Now would be good.

I tend to be a reasonable and rational skeptic. In fact, my good friend, Smitty, refers to me as the "Scully" to his "Mulder", making reference to the hit TV show, The X-Files. He leans toward wanting to believe most things are conspiratorial in nature, where I have a more rational approach. We make a good team. Neither of us trusts the government, so we have more in common than not. Since we both worked for the government, we feel we have the right not to trust them. They created the VA, after all.

CHAPTER FIVE: RESEARCH

"I believe there's too little patience and context to many of the investigations I read or see on television." – Bob Woodward

Contrary to what you may believe based on your extensive experience reading ground-breaking investigative reports by such pillars of journalism as InfoWars, WesternJournalism, DCClothesline, and AboveTopSecret, conducting a thorough and accurate investigation is difficult. It is time consuming and requires an analytical mind to be able to place each piece of the puzzle into its proper position. Sure, you can browse a few websites and gather some data, but that isn't going to get you to the truth any more than rubbing a rough stone against your forehead.

If the only source of your information is coming from questionable websites, all of which mysteriously link back to each other, you are setting yourself up for failure. For a proper perspective, you have to view both sides of the issue. Say what you will about mainstream media, but they are infinitely more reliable than the websites mentioned above. They are going to slant the coverage to fit their agenda but they don't typically *fabricate* stories out of whole cloth. In most cases, if you ignore the things that would be considered commentary within the article and just extract the factual statements, you can get a pretty good picture of what actually happened.

I will try to create such a scenario here. The following is a completely fabricated story that is slanted to suit an agenda. Totally fictitious. Trust me. Here we go –

Dateline Miami – Joe Schmoe, reporting.

The otherwise pleasant and picturesque Miami shoreline became a scene of violence, brutality, and death this afternoon following the police shooting of an Hispanic teenager near Jiffy Lube on Jones Street.

Hector Alesandro, whom witnesses say was unarmed at the time of the shooting, was killed by a hail of police bullets, killing him as he stood in the street. Witnesses told me that Hector was just licking an ice cream cone, minding his own business, standing in the middle of the intersection when police approached. Words were exchanged and then shots rang out, leaving Hector and his ruined cone on the sidewalk - both leaking obscenely into the gutter.

Police say Alesandro is a known felon, a gang

member, and was wanted for questioning in a series of gang-related shootings that occurred last month. Neighbors and friends tell a different story.

Anthony "Bling Bling" Torres, a long-time friend of Hector's, says the teenager had avoided most of the violence in their neighborhood and school. A good student, Hector had dreams of one day becoming a chemist and creating new, more effective pharmaceuticals.

"He wunt in no gang, or any stuff like dat. Dats all bull****, Holmes. He was my boy. Them pigs just shot him down in the street like a animal or some ****! He wudn't fightin' or runnin' or nutheen, Esse."

Community leaders described Hector as a helpful, and generous youngster who often made large donations to local charities, even though he didn't have a job.

Tensions are high here on Jones Street as community members gather to pay their respects to their lost friend, mourn the loss of another productive teenager, and express their anger at what they perceive as an increase in violence from the overly aggressive Miami police. Miami police have shot and killed more than 70 people between 1999 and 2013, a figure most leaders say is far too high.

Now, from this remarkable example of activist-journalism, how many facts can be extracted? Not many. This is what your typical online report, TV newscast, or newspaper column looks like today: A few facts mingled with a whole lot of conjecture and commentary. From this particular report, we can really only ascertain that Hector was a teenager and he was shot to death by police today. That's about it. We are given useless facts that are not pertinent to the incident, glowing epitaphs from friends of the deceased, and high-powered trigger words like "killing" and "aggressive." It's basically a hit piece on cops in Miami.

It will usually take days for any actual facts to leak out into the media. Facts like, Hector is 19 years old, not 15 or 14, which could easily be assumed because of the constant reference to a "teenager" and "young man" in the story. Hector's friend isn't going to start insulting his now deceased homey on live television so, he says nice things about him and tries to deflect any gang activity because that activity would probably implicate himself as well. So, days later when a lengthy criminal record and history of violence is revealed and it is determined that Hector was armed and reaching for his gun when he was killed, those facts will be too little and too late. The narrative has already been set in stone and anything that supports the police perspective will be rejected by a community filled with distrust of authority. Obviously, the police planted that evidence to cover up their murder of yet another young man of color.

This type of activism by journalists is incredibly dangerous. Not only does it violate what used to be called journalistic integrity, it is an active participation in creating the news, not reporting it. It's shameful and embarrassing and it happens every day. (Just watch MSNBC for an hour or so if you are looking for a real example.)

The result of this is that all of the keyboard sleuths hit all of these stories and then believe they have the truth. The truth takes time to develop and uncover, especially during an ongoing event or one that occurred just a few short hours ago. You have to wait for it. Jumping on the first reports to hit the airwaves and declaring it the factual, indisputable truth is both amateurish and naïve.

The best example I can think of is the conspiracy theorist's favorite: The secondary device.

In both Oklahoma City and the attacks on 9/11,

multiple people were quoted as saying there were secondary explosives. They were recorded, live, with cameras rolling, talking about it. This has become one of the most damning accusations from the conspiracy crowd when it comes to distrust of the official storyline.

For those unfamiliar, a secondary device would be a second explosive, or explosives, designed to detonate after the initial bomb blast. Often these devices are detonated as the emergency responders arrive on the scene in order to maximize the death toll. This tactic has been used all around the world and is believed to have originated with the Palestinians, who also tend to pack explosives into fake ambulances so they can get right up next to the emergency responders.

Here's the shocking truth about the matter – there were no secondary devices in Oklahoma or NYC. None. But, emergency responders, trained in responding to a terrorist attack and various bombing scenarios, are taught to be aware of the possibility and to assume there are secondary devices deployed in the attack. That way they aren't caught off guard by such a thing. They are trained to expect them and warn others of the possibility. I know this because I have been through the training myself. Since the possibility exists, you must warn others of it and operate under the correct procedures to prevent further disaster.

So, naturally, at the scene of any bomb attack on U.S. soil, you are going to find police, fire, and EMS officials mentioning and warning about secondary devices. People grab that, hold on for dear life, and push the notion that the government lied. Days, or even weeks later, when more facts surface and an actual analysis of the scene is completed, the official story clearly refutes the existence of any secondary device. But, since that story came from the government, we will ignore it and continue to talk about secondary devices and how they were obviously planted by the government itself in order to kill a bunch of people and blame it on sheep herders in order to go to war against another poor, innocent, third world nation. None of it is true, but it is the first thing people hear so it is hard to let it go.

If you think about it rationally, what purpose would it serve to have massive explosives secreted into the building - a feat that would take incredible resources, planning, and coordination – and then use a truck bomb to hit the building? None. If you could plant hidden bombs in the building, why bother with the truck bomb on the outside? You could just blow the bombs already inside the building and call it a day. The same is true of the WTC, "controlled demolition" theories that make me want to scratch someone's eyes out. It is ludicrous. The very idea is so ridiculous that you couldn't get an actual explosives expert or demo-man to even discuss the theory. It's always some Schmoe who has no actual experience in building demolition. The amount of explosives required, and the amount of time it would require to do a controlled demolition on even building 7 would take months to accomplish. And nobody was running into a burning building at the WTC complex carrying thousands of pounds of explosives while they burned and emergency responders were evacuating the victims. Who the hell even thinks up these ridiculous ideas anyway? It is the most absurd thing out there today and there is not one shred of evidence, not ONE, none, nada, nicht, to support it.

The same can be said of the frequent search for a "second shooter" during mass shooting events. It is the same principle. Responders are trained to not enter a scene with the assumption that there was only one shooter and they can let their guard down. The first priority is to ensure that the event is finished and all shooters are down, or have fled the scene. You never assume there was only one person. That is how people get killed as they arrive on scene. Okay, enough about that. Back to our regularly scheduled book.

Primacy is a training term we used when I was a military instructor. We broke it down to a simple phrase: First learned, best learned. The caveat was that if you train someone wrong the first time, it is very hard to alter that way of thinking because it is already embedded in their subconscious mind. So, teach them correctly the first time and you are doing your job as an instructor. All of you instructors out there who have ever had to "un-train" someone of all of the bad habits instilled in them by bad teachers will know exactly what I'm talking about. They learned the wrong thing but it was the first thing they learned about it and it takes time and effort to defeat that. Information is the same way. You will remember it. So then what if you stop remembering the follow-up information but retain that initial information? Ten years from now you are recounting a false narrative and fully believe it to be true. And it will be very difficult to convince you otherwise, regardless of the facts and evidence presented.

Conducting research is just like doing homework. Most people don't like doing it so they rely on others who they believe have done it for them. The only problem with that premise is that those other people probably didn't do it either. Even if they perform some level of research, you can almost always rest assured it was not painstakingly done. How deep was that research? Superficial – just by scanning a few websites? Or deep research – like actually going to the scene or searching through public documents databases and visiting the hall of records and making copies of real items? Maybe talking to a few people involved, even if done via email? Now, think back. How many "news items" do you read every day that include the phrase, "not immediately available for comment" or "did not immediately respond to our request for an interview"? Probably quite a few. I read a few today myself.

What does that mean? It means I'm a lazy reporter with a deadline to meet (which isn't usually true today since reporters can post their articles directly to the organization's website sans editor) and I wasn't going to wait for the other side of the story before putting my totally unbiased and balanced article in the public arena. That, my friends, is exactly what it means. What, they called, got voice mail, hung up, and then inserted that "cover my ass" phrase into their article? Yep. Pretty much.

Nothing else explains why someone would post an article about a conflict between two people and only speak to one person, or neither person. That isn't journalism. That is writing an opinion piece. You might as well be Dear Abby at that point because you aren't actually reporting news using insightful, investigative journalism.

You have to think like a detective. If you have never been a detective, which is the situation in which most people find themselves, you can do a passable impersonation with very little effort. Most of the so-called detectives you see as guests on evening news programs have been getting away with it for years so it can work for you as well.

The first thing you have to do is put on some weight. I don't know why. It's just a thing. Once you are promoted from beat cop to detective, the next day you wake up and realize you have put on thirty pounds. Maybe it's the donuts? The same is true for private investigators. The weight magically appears upon receiving your license. There are exceptions, of course, like Thomas Magnum, but he was in Hawaii and had a reputation to maintain.

Next, you have to drink coffee. Lots of coffee. If you are currently a regular coffee drinker, at a minimum, you will have to triple your daily intake of coffee.

The third thing you have to do is realize that

everyone is going to lie to you about something in some form or fashion. It may be a small lie, or a large lie, but they will lie. And get this, sometimes they don't even realize they are lying. It is your job to figure it out. That's why you're the detective.

Another important tip is that the best detectives don't work alone. Holmes has his Watson. Charlie Chan has his number one son. And Simon had the other Simon. It is important to have another detective or otherwise qualified person, such as your wife, review your work. Few detectives that I have ever known have begun an investigation, completed an investigation, and forwarded those findings to the powers that be completely unaided. It doesn't matter how experienced you are, you can always miss something. Having a fresh set of eyes on the information can be a huge help. I am fortunate to be surrounded by others who are experienced investigators also. I rarely ever even post a blog post without someone else seeing it prior to its submission.

An example from my recent past is the case we will call, "The Case of the Three Armed Robber." In that case, it wasn't until the defendant's appeal from his conviction that anyone noticed that in order for him to have accomplished the heinous crime, he must have had three arms. He supposedly used one arm to extract a woman from a car, while simultaneously ripping the car door open with his other arm, and holding a gun on her with his other other arm. The frightening thing about this particular case is that it was only realized during the appeal. Which means, the beat cop, the detective, the prosecutor, the defense attorney, and the jury (because this was a jury trial) all failed to realize that fact.

The bottom line is that anyone can miss a piece of the puzzle or neglect to make mention of a piece of the puzzle in their recitation of the events. If you simply forget to include a seemingly simple aspect of the event, you aren't relaying the full picture to your audience. Details are important, and occasionally, they are critical. In the case above, the information about the three arms didn't necessarily indicate that the defendant was not guilty, but at a minimum it meant another guilty party was still free to commit more crimes. Perhaps he only had one arm.

DEVELOPING THE QUESTIONS

We have all heard the description of, "Who, What, When, Where, Why, and How?" If you follow that simple guidance, it will get you pretty far. If your source of information only partially covers the WWWWWH guideline, then you have more work to do. Document research is critical in this regard. Gather as much collateral information – information from any source outside of the original documentation – as possible. Give yourself as many perspectives on the event as can be gained.

Compare all of the various versions of events.

Sometimes this involves making a list. Yes, there are lists. Lots of lists. You have to keep notes, lists, and various structural outlines of the information so you can keep it straight in your head while you are attempting to solve the riddle. Something as simple as a peripheral date surrounding some aspect of the event might prove to be invaluable if you find that it relates to some other piece of the puzzle. But, if you didn't write it down, you aren't going to put those two things together. There is a reason serious case files wind up being several inches thick. Some take up entire file cabinets. Once you have all of the information you can obtain, make a timeline of the events. That timeline needs to include all of the various perspectives.

In your timeline, you not only need to attempt to ascertain who, what, when, where, why, and how, but also who was where, when, doing what, how, and why. In doing so, you may find that some of those witnesses were not witnesses at all. Now you can put their statements in the trash because you don't want that inaccurate information sullying your investigation.

Compare the statements to the known facts of the events. You should start to see a picture emerging about the situation in general. Then you keep going. As I said, conducting a thorough investigation takes time and effort.

I have no intention to author an investigations guide. That has been done by many more qualified people than me. Sheila L. Stephens, my friend and fellow seeker of the truth, for instance. Her book, The Everything Private Investigation Book, is a best seller and a copy is even in a museum somewhere. So, let's get down to brass tacks here.

Stop trusting people. That is as good a place to start as any. Just because one of your favorite political figures, actors, comedians, or some seemingly intelligent, anonymous website posts something to Facebook, Twitter, or anywhere else on the web, doesn't mean it is true. In fact, in most cases, if it is true at all, it is generally only partially true. Take the five minutes to double check the information before mindlessly spreading it and perpetuating the myth. Sometimes those famous people were fooled in the same way you were. It's like a plague.

If you can't get your hands on any factual information – actual evidence – then you have to remain militantly agnostic, which means you don't know. If you don't know, how can you actually hold an opinion on the subject? We should all believe things because they are true, not because we wish they were true.

Remember the old adage, "If it sounds too good to be true, it probably is"? Remember that the next time a story crosses your screen that seems to perfectly satisfy everything you want to believe is true. Obama is an illegal immigrant, Muslim, antichrist? Yeah, you might want to do a little research yourself before clicking that "share" button. If you don't, you will make yourself look either foolish, or like a complete ass. If you are okay with that, then you are beyond my help.

CHAPTER SIX: JUST STOP

"A great many people think they are thinking when they are merely rearranging their prejudices." – William James

The purpose of this book was two-fold: To encourage people to think for themselves, and to help them not make fools of themselves in public. And, well, perhaps have a few laughs along the way. I hope I satisfied those goals. Both the book and this chapter are titled, Just Stop, because that is what more people need to say to themselves on a daily basis. Just stop.

Stop jumping on the bandwagon of every

extreme point of view just because it fits within your preconceived notions or prejudices. Yes, we all have those. They aren't necessarily racial in nature, but we all have prejudices. Perhaps we hate hippies, so everything that is anti-hippie is immediately accepted whether or not there is any truth to it. Perhaps we hate Muslims because we see them as the source of the violence and misery we call terrorism. Therefore, calling someone a Muslim, or Muslim sympathizer becomes a form of ultimate insult. Some people are still hung up on the old standby of black and white relations. Whatever the predisposition of your prejudices, you need to recognize them for the powerful influence they are. You may not even realize you have them.

If you want to be a force for good in this world, and not a divisive, angry agitator, the first step is to stop. Before you move that mouse cursor or issue your well-thought out (usually just the opposite) comment, remove your fingers from the keyboard, sit up straight, and stop for a few moments. Then think. Think before you act. When you do act, make it meaningful. Do the research. Find some answers. Dig up some actual facts. Then, and only then, should you hold an opinion on the subject. That still doesn't mean you are going to impress anyone when you decide to express that opinion but, at least people might believe you have studied the issue instead of learning all about it on InfoWars.

Approach every situation from a position of neutrality. Learn the facts and review the evidence. Let the information sway your position on the subject, not your prejudices or desires. Others will see your prejudices whether you see them or not. It will be present in everything you share and every comment you make. You can be a productive part of the conversation, or you can become a subject of ridicule. The choice is yours.

We as a society have to learn that not everything is a product of someone's agenda. Not every thug who is shot by police was unarmed and had his hands up. In fact, you may have to dig for quite a while to find a case like that. The fact that it is so unheard of, so outrageous of an accusation, should have been a red flag to anyone hearing the story. But, instead of the populace thinking, "Hey, wait a minute. That doesn't seem like something that would happen every day. Shoot an unarmed man who has his hands up in the middle of the street in broad daylight in front of dozens of witnesses?"

But, that isn't what a large segment of our population did. Nope. They ran with the erroneous story from the lying shoplifter with a criminal record who had just helped that now deceased man rob a convenience store. Yep, that's who we should rely upon for our most accurate information. The story fit the narrative just too neatly. White cops oppress, abuse, and murder black people. That's what a large section of our population are taught to believe, and so that simple lie was easy for them to swallow. It fit with their prejudices.

To ensure this topic isn't one sided, the same thing often happens on the other end of the spectrum. How many people have been sent to prison, or even the electric chair (just as an example since we don't actually fry people anymore) and then we later learned they were innocent of that crime? It is more than you want to believe. Hundreds. Thousands. Perhaps tens of thousands during the course of our legal system's existence. Do you know why? People looked at the situation and, based on their prejudices, said, "Yep. I can totally see that happening. He even looks like a murderer." When you view situations from that position, the weight of the evidence has to be pretty substantial to change your position. Sometimes no amount is enough.

There are serious problems in the world today. There are real and provable conspiracies in the world today. There is no need to create false issues in order to enrage or incite others. There is plenty going on about which you should be angry. Why push fiction into the mix? Find something real; something you've investigated and proven to yourself using real evidence and factual data. Run with it! Make a difference. At this point, you are only making a mess.

People who create the false narrative, push the erroneous outrage, and create fictional conspiracies in order to frighten people are no different than the very boogeymen they want you to fear. They are creating monsters to occupy dark spaces under your beds in order to relieve you of your hard-earned dollars. They also cause very real pain for those involved in the situations around which the conspiracy theory is formed.

Can you imagine, just for one second, what it must feel like for a parent of one of the victims of the Sandy Hook school shooting to flip through their Facebook newsfeed and be greeted by imaginary "proof" that their lost child wasn't really killed? That those children are still happy and healthy and in hiding because it was all a government run false flag operation in order to do whatever it is those idiots think they do? Can you even conceive of what that must feel like as you look to your fireplace mantle and shed tears yet again over the loss of your beloved child?

Or to see and hear idiotic statements about the passengers on the airplanes hijacked during 9/11 and how they weren't actually on the planes and they were all government agents who are now living it up on an island with George Bush? What kind of mental disorder do you have to possess in order to take joy in producing that kind of pain in others? It is despicable. How would it make you feel?

I will tell you.

A few years ago, some friends of mine were killed during our combat tour in Afghanistan. In that incident, the media were present and it resulted in many photos, and even video, hitting the internet within minutes of the incident. We tried to get the photos out of the public eye but we couldn't stop them all and some of them are still out there. I occasionally see them cross my feeds on social media. Sometimes it is a "remember them" type of post but, at other times, it is an anti-military rant that accompanies the photo. One day the accompanying rant was, and I will paraphrase, the following:

"Look at this fake photo trying to promote a hero narrative for our murderers overseas! This photo is totally fake. That isn't even real blood. Blood isn't that red. This was totally staged, false flag bullshit so you ignorant, war-loving Americans will keep supporting 'the troops.' And you'll fall for it because you are a bunch of sheeple."

How did it make me feel, seeing my friends' dead bodies displayed for everyone to see and then having them insulted and degraded in such a manner? I wanted to kill that little jackass. And I probably would have if he was anywhere near me. I wanted to reach through the screen and choke the life out of him for his ignorance. And those were just my friends. If that was my child, I probably would have employed my investigative skill toward finding him just so I could smash his sweaty, pimple-covered face into a wall.

I'm sure thousands of people bought in to his ridiculous conspiracy theory garbage. Hell, for all I know, he has his own radio show. Lies are popular. They always have been. Lies make money. The truth, well, the truth never made anyone rich. The truth shall set you free, but freedom doesn't pay the bills.

After taking a couple of days to calm down, I emailed the offending poster and asked that he remove the photo from his page. I provided a lengthy explanation of the request. He did remove it and offered an apology for the offense. I don't know if he has since changed his mind about his previous conduct or if he is still hard at work creating false ideas in order to garner attention. I stopped caring after our email exchange. I hope I had a positive effect on him. I am not optimistic. He probably removed the photo out of fear.

So, don't be that guy. Don't be the one who gets the quick email from Ross Elder or his Truth Crusade Investigations Team informing you that, "You have just been added to the target list." You'll be given a chance to make the situation right but, if you persist in your ignorance, well, I guess we will make you famous and tell the world just how wrong you are. And we'll call you names. Lots of silly names.

So, just….. stop.

Just stop.

THE END

ABOUT THE AUTHOR

Ross Elder is a freelance writer, occasional journalist, voice-over actor, novelist, military veteran, and self-proclaimed guardian of internet truth. He is a former professional investigator for both law enforcement and corporate organizations. A disabled combat veteran, Ross lives in the Midwest United States with his wife and children.

OTHER BOOKS BY ROSS ELDER

THE FIREMAN
BOOK ONE
UNHINGED
MERCS
COMPENDIUM (THE FIREMAN COLLECTION)

And, coming soon…

THE OLD ONES – A new novel

And…

The next installment in the Fireman Saga series –
working title, Book Two

KEEP UP TO DATE BY VISITING
ROSS-ELDER.COM